Harvesting Pigs at Home

Traditional Methods, Exceptional Results

Table of Contents

Forward: Why would you want to do this?

"Why in the world would you want to do that?" It is one of the first questions you will face if you start voicing interest in exploring a more personal involvement with the harvesting of a pig. Though there are cultures today that still practice traditional harvest methods, the days of hands-on work of this kind are not a part of our collective memory in America. Even in rural areas, the work of raising a pig might still be practiced, but slaughter and butchery are left in the hands of others. For those who raise pigs for the purpose of making products available for retail sale, regulations dictate this division of labor. But for many others, this is simply the result of the "way things are."

Fortunately this status quo has been coming under more intense scrutiny as people begin to reevaluate their relationship with the food systems of our contemporary culture. A growing dissatisfaction with the quality and safety of food produced in an industrial model is leading to a new willingness to explore local sources for fruit, vegetables and even meat. Home gardens, CSAs, and farmers' markets are giving people a new perspective on our relationship to food. This welcome change has led to a desire to reclaim and remember old, forgotten skills, like gardening, canning, pickling and preserving. Among those forgotten skills are traditional methods of harvesting a pig.

Keith and I met in 2010 and quickly discovered we shared a concern for providing our families with food we could trust. Neither of us had a background in agriculture, but both of us believed that anything could be done with a little research and lot of effort. Access to a small, run-down farm property gave us a place to start experimenting. We began with a chicken coop, as many do, and immediately enjoyed the benefits of having fresh farm eggs available. A garden quickly followed and we were able to take some more items off our families' shopping lists. Some beehives on the property helped with the garden and provided honey. At every step we found that what we grew for ourselves was of a quality that far outpaced any grocery-store counterparts. And we also learned that the work involved was fun (most of the time!) and satisfying.

As our confidence grew with experience, we began to talk about raising a few pigs on the farm for the purpose of providing a range of pork products to our families. This was a far more intimidating task and we found precious little information available to help us get started. Our research yielded plenty of information on the raising of pigs, but the process of harvest was most often left in the hands of professionals. The norm seemed to be to either transport the pigs to a facility or to have them killed by appointment on your property, after which the carcasses would be transported to a butcher. A week or two later the wrapped and labeled pork products would be available.

While this remains a suitable option for many, we felt we wanted to take a more hands-on approach. It took a great deal of research to compile all the necessary information. We wanted to be sure that we were utilizing the very best and humane practices with our animals and that the resulting products would be safe for consumption by our families. What we found is that the task of home harvest is not only achievable, but also incredibly rewarding. It makes sense in so many practical ways (reduced cost, increased yield, control of end product), and we were also surprised by other benefits, including the way the process cultivates community, inspires generosity, and imparts a profound respect and appreciation for the animals involved.

For those with economy in mind, the pig is a great choice for getting the most out of your dollar. It is possible to get the price-per-pound cost of your harvest down into really impressive territory – but total cost will be a combination of many factors outside of the purview of this book (the present suitability of your existing facilities, your ability to creatively resource feed, etc.). We would caution those who are looking for the cheapest pork chop or bacon to take a moment to evaluate the full range of reasons that might inspire you to take up this work for yourselves. There is much more to be gained than simply a lower price for pork at the end of the day.

This book is the result of our research and our practical experience. It is our hope that the advice and procedures collected here will be of great help to anyone who is contemplating taking on this task for the first time. We do not claim that what is described here is THE way to approach this process, but we can attest that it is a very good way. Our hope is that you will find these materials helpful as you consider this choice for yourself.

The Pig

Raising a pig is the first step towards harvesting one. There is a wealth of information available the help you determine what kind of pig to raise and how to humanely raise it, so we will only give some very general advice. A pig is a near-perfect animal for those contemplating raising and harvesting their own meat for the first time. They can be raised with relatively little space, they are generally hardy, intelligent and full of personality. A pig purchased as a "weaner" (meaning that the piglet has been weaned from the mother) will grow to suitable weight (220-320lbs) in as little as four months. So a piglet bought in May could well be ready for harvest in October. This is a manageable commitment of time, especially for those who have not raised and cared for larger animals before.

The experience of buying a piglet will vary greatly region by region, so advice here will be extremely generalized. First, research the breed of pig you may be interested in raising. This is not a question with a "right" answer, instead you should familiarize yourself broadly with breed types so you can make some informed choices when presented with real, live piglets for sale. Pig breeds that are favored by commercial markets tend towards quick growth and leanness of carcass, this includes breeds like the Yorkshire and the

Duroc. While these breeds, well cared for, will yield excellent product, they offer little in the way of fat, which, it turns out, is one of the great benefits of the noble pig. In a bygone era, products derived from pork fat were much valued in the American diet, but as shortening replaced lard and leanness became the primary characteristic looked for in meat (often at the sacrifice of flavor and quality), fat became a dirty word. There are still breeds available in the United States that offer a better ratio of meat-to-fat, they often go by the name of "heritage breed", their lines being preserved by the careful work of small farms that remember their value. Breeds like Mangalitsa, Berkshire and Tamworth are finding their way back into markets as chefs and home cooks alike rediscover the phenomenal flavor and value they offer.

You may find that your area tends to have certain kinds of breeds available – whatever is common will be less expensive. You may want to choose a heritage breed, in which case you will have to work a little harder to find a source. In rural, semi-rural, or even suburban areas, Craigslist is a great resource for finding piglets for sale. Be sure to check out the conditions they are being raised in before committing to a purchase. Livestock auctions in your area will often have pigs on their lists, especially in the spring (start searching for an auction house near you). Farm supply stores may have a bulletin board for posting for-sale notices from local farmers.

One of the considerations for when to buy a piglet is the projected date of harvest. Traditionally, pig harvest is done during the fall or winter, when outside temperatures are low enough (below 40 degrees) to allow the processing to happen outdoors without danger of the meat spoiling. In our case, we generally aim to have our pigs at their finished weight by the end of October or early November, when temperatures in our area are reliably cool. Harvesting a pig in warmer climates presents a challenge, and options like a cold-room should be explored. We have built a cold room, which extends our harvest abilities – information about the fabrication of this very useful tool can be found in the appendix. In either case, working backwards from your ideal harvest dates will help determine when to purchase your piglets.

Pigs are very intelligent and social animals and will thrive if raised with companions. Consider purchasing and raising a minimum of two animals, perhaps with the investment of friends or family. Provide adequate, secure space, shelter, clean water and a ready supply of food (you will be amazed at their rate of consumption as they grow!). They are a lot of fun to watch and play with, until they start putting on real weight and size. Our kids enjoyed coming in to help feed the piglets and give them a scratch on the ear or belly, but there came a time when we restricted access because of concerns for safety. Use good common sense and exercise caution when feeding and caring for these animals.

Pigs are omnivorous and will happily consume a wide variety of foods. You can raise them on hog feed, either metering the food out or allowing them to feed at will. Some people raise their pigs primarily on pasture (yes, pigs can graze their way to greatness) and supplement with some grain. Others feed their pigs dairy and eggs, gathered from other animals on their property. Gardens can yield all kinds of goodies that the pigs will love – you will finally have a place for all those zucchini your friends hand out in the summer! Groundfall fruit is great for the mix, and the fall is a good season for finding pumpkins cheap or free. Remember that you are raising meat for your own consumption, so do not feed the pigs garbage or food leftovers you wouldn't eat yourself. Leverage your particular resources to keep your pigs and your pocketbook happy and you will be amazed at how they will put the weight on.

There are a lot of opinions about what size is the "right" size for harvesting a pig. Generally speaking, a pig is ready to be harvested at about 220lbs, but we have harvested pigs as large as 380lbs. Such a size difference can greatly impact the process of harvest – a larger animal needs a larger scald tank, heartier equipment to handle and hold the carcass, and more hands to move around. But a larger animal also yields thicker bacon, more back fat, thicker chops, etc. At a certain point the animals will continue to pile on the pounds but mostly in more fat, not muscle mass. This means feed costs continue to rise but total yield doesn't – the numbers just don't pan out. In our experience the ideal weight is something in the neighborhood of 280-300lbs – this gives a good balance of meat and fat and some truly impressive bacon. When your pigs are in a range acceptable to you, it is time to get ready to harvest.

Tools & Equipment

In the world of home pig harvest there is a watershed decision that will greatly impact the kinds of tools and equipment you will need: to skin or to scald. Some folks opt to skin the hog after it is killed, working with a carcass that is devoid of that hardy protective layer. We have opted to pursue a more traditional method, what is known as the "scald and scrape" process. This leaves the skin intact on the carcass, which makes the carcass extremely easy to move around, and is a great help during butchering. There are other benefits as well, which we will cover later in this book. We probably deliberated more over this decision than almost any other as we prepared to harvest our first pigs – though it involves a great deal of work, we are firmly convinced that the resulting products are superior in many ways.

Much of our tool and equipment list is particular to this method, as are, of course, our instructions for harvest.

We have grouped the required equipment by task so that you will have a sense of where it all fits in the process:

The Kill:

.22 caliber rifle & ammo

Large sanitized bowl or bucket for blood collection
Whisk
Quart canning jars for blood storage
Strainer
Long-bladed knife for "sticking"
Supply of clean water
Brushes for cleaning carcass
Gambrel with 500lb capacity

The Scald:

Something to raise the carcass above scalding tank – a forklift is especially handy, but a come-along and frame/tree can do the trick just as well.

55-110 gallon Scalding Tank
High BTU propane burner
Propane tank
Thermometer to track water temp
Supply of clean water

The Scrape:

2-3 Bell Scrapers (available at ButcherPacker.com)
Razor-sharp knives (boning knives work well)
Brillo pads for final scrub
Supply of clean water

Evisceration:

Frame to hang carcasses
Twine
Selection of knives (more on this below)
Bone saw/reciprocating saw with fine-tooth blade

Several sterile bus tubs
Large, heavy-duty garbage bags

Supply of warm water
Wash, sterilize, and rinse stations (bus tubs work well)
Towels
Heavy-duty steel s-hooks (available at
ButcherPacker.com)
Sharpening steel
2-3 long tables
Bourbon & shot glasses (optional)

Most of the equipment is fairly self-explanatory, but there are a couple of items that deserve more discussion. Specific recommendations of tools and equipment can be found at our resource site www.harvestingathome.net.

Scalding Tank

The Scalding Tank is the container that will hold the hot water for scalding the pig prior to scraping. It needs to be large enough to hold at least one half of the length of a full-grown pig, with enough room left for hot water to circulate freely. One of the most conveniently available types of container is the

55-gallon drum, which can often be found around farm properties or on Craigslist for a very reasonable price. These steel drums, once cleaned, are adequate for pigs in the 200lb-230lb range. If your animals are much larger than this, you will find a larger tank much more convenient. Finding a larger tank, however, can present something of a challenge. Call scrap yards, search through local classifieds, or just keep your eyes peeled for vertical tanks that look to be large enough to do the trick. Keith was able to spot an old 110-gallon water tank on a property that he passed one day, and the owner was happy to have him haul it away for a few dollars. He cut the top with a plasma torch and installed a ball valve at the bottom for drainage. A little bit of paint to clean it up and we became the proud owners of a tank that was ideal, even for hogs weighing in close to 400lbs. A good scald tank will serve for many seasons of harvest, so we recommend taking time to find one that will work for the widest range of sizes.

Knives, etc.

There are really only a few knives and tools necessary to successfully harvest and break down an entire pig in a home setting. Those few knives should be sharpened and honed to a near-surgical edge – taking time to learn to accomplish this will serve this task and many others. This list is more than sufficient for all the tasks you'll face:
6" boning knife (stiff or flexible are both fine) – you can use this knife for the "stick", for scraping/shaving hair off the carcass, as well as during various stages of evisceration and butchering.
10"-12" straight steak or cimeter knife – this large blade will find the most use during butchery, but it is also

handy for removal of the head from the carcass on harvest day.

3"-4" paring or skinning knife – a small blade is very handy for parts of the evisceration task, as well as for a few random tasks associated with the scald and scrape.

Bone saw – don't settle for saws used for breaking down big game, they will not give good results. A fine-toothed bone saw will get plenty of use for evisceration and for butchering – don't skimp on this important tool. You can find them online at butcherpacker.com and other locations. We have now had experience with several models and can attest that the higher the quality of the tool, the better the results.

Specific tools for the task

There are a few tools that are specific to this kind of work that may not be familiar to you, but are essential for making the day go smoothly.

gambrel – it looks something like a strong, steel coat hanger. It is meant to hang a whole animal carcass while keeping the legs spread apart (convenient for evisceration). You'll want one that is rated for at least 500lbs. Outdoor suppliers that serve big-game hunters are a good place to look, as are butcher supply outlets like butcherpacker.com.

stainless steel s-hook – This is one of those things that is common to the meat-processing world, but not readily available in your local hardware store. Don't settle for substitutes, having several of these heavy-duty hooks available will make the job much easier. They are available at ButcherPacker.com, listed as an "8-inch stainless steel s-hook," and they are sturdy enough to handle your largest animal.

Bell scraper – This strange tool consists of a round, concave disk affixed to a handle, looking something like the bottom half of a candlestick. In fact, old time homesteaders used candlesticks, sharpening the bottom edges and drawing out a burr before applying them to the task of scraping. This tool has one job – to rapidly scrape the scurf (the top layer of skin that is removed after scalding) off the pig. The first challenge is to find one – antique and used versions sometimes pop up on places like eBay or sit unidentified in antique stores. New models are available at butcherpacker.com. The second challenge is to put it someplace where you can find it the next time you need it!

Frame for evisceration

You will need a place to hang the carcass in order to work on it. Ideally this will be located near the area you have chosen to set up your scalding tank. A frame can be constructed from wood or steel that can be set up temporarily and then put away for the rest of the year. Keith is handy with a welder and put together a frame from scrap metal that was lying around the farm and shop. With a steel i-beam as the backbone, the frame was constructed to be set up and taken down with relative ease, and is strong enough and long enough to hold four whole carcasses. Something like that is probably overkill for most situations, but we sure find it convenient when we are working to process more than one animal in a day. Whether working in wood or metal, carefully consider your design - you must be confident that it can hold the weight and it must suspend the carcass at a height convenient to work on. For some folks this will amount to a chain or rope thrown over a sturdy branch on a tree – others will have to engineer a solution.

Space

Not everyone has a great deal of flexibility in this regard, but here are a few considerations for the space where you will be working. We have found that the easiest way to accomplish the kill with the very least amount of stress to the animal is to kill the animal in the space the animal is most comfortable in. This will usually be the pen, pasture, or paddock where they have been raised. The processing area should be reasonably close to this site so the carcass does not need to be moved a great deal. Take a moment to consider lines of sight around the work area and take care to ensure that neighbors or passers-by will not be unwittingly exposed to a view of the work. It is a natural and ordinary process, but the sight of a pig carcass in various stages of disassembly can come as an unwelcome surprise to the unprepared. You don't want to have the local school bus drive by with a full view of you shoulder deep in a dismembered pig.

A little planning with an eye towards workflow will help make the day go smoothly. If you are using equipment like a forklift or tractor you will want to make sure there are clear lanes for the movement of those machines, giving special concern to any traffic around the scalding tank. Ready access to clean water is also a consideration. It may be that your site has hot and cold water available – if not, you can set up a large pot on a propane burner to keep a supply of hot water going throughout the day. A firm and level spot for the scalding tank is a must. We enjoyed working in an outdoor setting, but one is subject to weather conditions, of course.

We like to set up several long tables so that we have surfaces available to hold tools and knives, wash stations, and to provide work areas for specific jobs like "head work", which will be described later. Having needful items close at hand means there is little wasted time, especially during critical tasks.

Considerations of all of these factors, of the animals, water sources, vehicle access, and protection from the elements, etc., may, at times, be in conflict with one another. When in doubt, always defer to the safest solutions and think through what would be the most humane manner to deal with the animals. The rest will fall into place. Remember that it is not necessary that one site be equipped for all the tasks of harvest. Butchering can easily be done at another site that is better suited for the work.

Community

There is more work to be done at the harvest than can be done by one person. This is one of the reasons, perhaps, that these skills have  disappeared from contemporary life. Our modern food system makes individual portions readily available to us and this allows us to maintain our isolation from our neighbors.

Traditionally, the harvest of a pig was a community affair, bringing together friends and family to share in the labor and to share in the bounty that the pig provides. A bare minimum of 2 people could conceivably get the job done, but 5-6 people can easily be accommodated at the worksite, taking turns in tasks like scraping, or working to keep workstations clean and well organized.

We have found that people are genuinely curious about this process and recruiting helping hands has never proven to be a problem. Planning for the involvement of friends and family is part of the process. We have found that labor is usually happily offered in exchange for beer and the value of the experience itself. A break during the work for pork tacos (the hanging skirt is a tender cut of meat easily accessed on harvest day) will keep people motivated.

Interest is hardly limited to "farm types" – urban and suburban life can create a real longing in folks to connect more closely with food and with authentic experiences of harvest. The involvement of a community of people at harvest is not simply a requirement of the job – it is one of the greatest benefits of taking on this work for yourself.

Preparing for the kill

The idea of taking the life of an animal you have raised is often one of the most significant hurdles for people who are considering harvesting animals at home. It is natural to feel reluctance and anxiety. But fully confronting this aspect of harvest is an important part of the responsibility we bear when we choose to consume pork products in our home. To face the death of the animal reminds us of the cost of our consumption and increases our respect for the animal and the sense of value we have for the whole of what the animal provides. This is what informs the ethos of nose-to-tail eating – no part of the animal is left to waste, for to adopt a casual attitude towards what we are eating would be out of place. It is all useful; not only useful but incredibly healthful and delicious, and we have a responsibility to use it well. We came to the conclusion that taking responsibility for the death of the animal was a natural extension of our responsibility to raise and care for it.

Once you have come to terms with the choice to take the responsibility to kill your animal, you will want to focus on the best way to accomplish the task. Safety is of the highest order, followed closely by concern for the humane treatment of your animals. We devised several complex plans for isolating the pigs from one another and moving them into "kill pens" that were located close to our scalding tank. All of those plans fell apart as soon as we tried to get the pigs to cooperate with them. Pigs, like other herd animals, are suspicious of new routines and new spaces. They are not likely to just trot into a space they have never been in before, nor are they going to be excited about leaving behind any companions. All actions taken to get them to conform to such plans will inevitably stress the animals and the owners. It turns out the simplest solution is usually the best, and this is certainly the case in this instance.

We found that the pigs are most easily killed in their own pen. In order to get ready for the day, keep the pigs off food and water for 12 hours before the kill (some folks like to withhold food for 24 hours in order to have the bowels relatively empty). The pigs can be given a bowl full of a mash made of water, corn and chopped apples, which they will happily turn their attention to, and the shooter can then line up the shot while the pig is occupied with their last meal. We have not seen any anxiety in their companions when the pigs are killed in a pen with others present. Keeping the other pigs occupied with corn or apples will allow the first stages of work to be accomplished quickly and in relative peace.

Before the shot occurs, there needs to be a team assembled that is clear on the tasks that will happen immediately after the pig falls. We have found it is very useful to have 3-4 people ready to jump in after the shooter's job is accomplished. One person is assigned the job of "sticker", another one or two will assist with rolling the pig onto its side and holding it during the blood collection process, and yet another is responsible for collecting the blood (which will be used for blood sausage). This team will stand behind the shooter and be ready to jump in once it is safe for them to do so.

When the jobs are assigned, the people ready, and the pig is feeding on its last meal, it is time to take the shot.

Taking the Shot

It is safe to say that Keith and I obsessed about this moment in the process for several months before our first harvest day. We were both concerned that the moment of death be quick and humane. We discovered clear and sometimes sobering examples of how NOT to do this (the internet can be a scary place) and took time to study the concepts behind a "good" kill. Brandon Sheard of farmsteadmeatsmith.com, an artisan butcher and abattoir located in the Pacific Northwest, summed up the concern we had when he told us:

"You only have to make a mistake on this once to ensure that you will never want to make a mistake again."

The obvious goal is to quickly and humanely kill the pig. This is best done by shooting the pig with a .22 caliber long-rifle shell, which, when rightly placed, will instantly render the pig senseless. A knife is then used to cut the main arteries in the neck and the pig will bleed out (this blood can be collected and preserved). Done correctly, the process takes several minutes.

In our research, Keith and I were exposed to a variety of other methods and, unfortunately, to the range of possible outcomes that result when the job is poorly done. No one who has invested the time, attention, and care into their animals to bring them up to the point of harvest would want to subject those animals to suffering or stress. There are practical considerations as well: the meat of a stressed animal will take on off flavors, the result of physiological responses in the pig before death. Taking special care to ensure a quick and humane kill is not simply a moral responsibility, it is also good economy. Fortunately a good result is not particularly difficult to achieve – you simply want to take every precaution to ensure that you achieve it….every time.

The physiology of the pig provides the best clues to help you place the killing shot. A pig's skull is well designed for a pig's life. They are rooters, diggers and their bodies are designed to make them very good at it – large neck muscles and sturdy snout allow them to plow up to 18" deep as they root for tasty treats in their pasture. An incredibly strong and thick skull plate at the front of the head strengthens and protects their brain cavity. A .22 caliber rifle fired into this strong skull plate will NOT be able to penetrate to the brain. At best the pig will not even notice such a misplaced shot, that's how strong the skull plate is. At worst, the pig will become wounded and alarmed. At this point the kill has gotten a lot more complicated.

Fortunately there is a thin spot in the front of the skull where a .22 caliber shell can easily penetrate to the brain. This is the spot that you MUST find when lining up your shot. It can be found by imagining an "X" drawn across the front of the pigs head, lines crossing from the left eye to the right ear, and the right eye to the left ear. The proper spot is not where the lines cross, but slightly above that point. The proper angle is required to ensure that the shell penetrates to the brain, rather than passing in front of, behind, or beside it. Standing directing in front of the pig, the shot should be aimed straight along the body, imagining a line running from nose to tail, and should be directed at a very slight downward angle. A solid understanding of these concepts is required of the shooter in order to ensure that the job gets done. It is not enough to simply "shoot the pig in the head" – the shot must find the proper location. Take time in the weeks leading up to your slaughter date to examine the area and be sure of your target.

It is obviously a help to the shooter when the pig is keeping still. One of the few times that a pig will keep their head still is when they are drinking, which is why we recommend that their last meal be a liquid mash (we use water, corn and chopped apples). The pig will then give you a brief window of cooperation. This is the moment when you want to 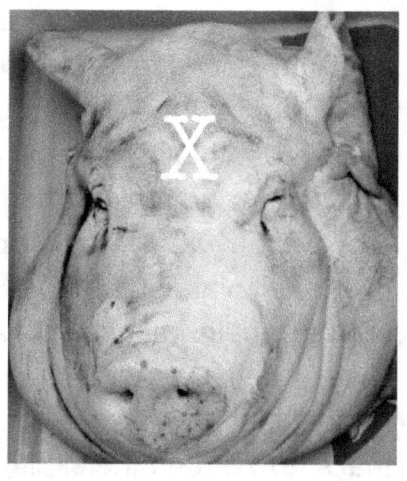 make sure that you take the time to do the job right. There is no need to rush the shot, there is no need to take the shot if the right conditions do not present themselves. Take a breath, and come at the situation again. The shot can be lined up at point-blank range or further away, but do not press the barrel to the pig's head as this can result in a dangerous misfire.

Safety for the shooter and others is of the highest priority. Be aware of where the gun is pointed at all times, ensure that there is no one waiting "downrange" of the shooter's position. Make sure that other animals, if present, are not in a position to jostle the shooter or otherwise interfere with the shot. Have a plan for securing the gun after the shot so that it does not get placed in a compromising position, loaded and unsecured, during the hustle and bustle that will follow. This is especially important if there are kids in the area. We like to make sure that the shooter has one focus and is not needed for the quick work that will follow. That way they can make sure the gun is properly stowed after the shot has been delivered.

You can do this. Take your time, line up the correct angles, and when the moment presents itself, take the shot. Doing this job well is part of the responsibility we owe to the animals that we are harvesting – they provide us with the means of life, but at the expense of theirs.

All this being said, it may be that something goes wrong and you find yourself with an animal that is wounded and suffering. Your unavoidable responsibility is to finish the job. You may be able to place another shot, but do not simply fire again in hope of hitting something – make sure that you can make it work, or the situation will only get worse. You must assess the state of affairs and calmly come to a new plan – don't rush into another mistake. Most likely you will be able to slowly, carefully, find opportunity to line up another shot – it may take some time, but you must persist. Maintain caution as the animals are incredibly strong and when wounded may act unpredictably. You have started a process that you must see through to the end.

When done correctly, the pig's body will go rigid and drop instantly and relatively quietly (a wounded pig will cry out and needs to be dispatched). The bullet has lodged into the brain and caused mortal trauma – the animal is now senseless, and you can proceed quickly with the next steps.

The "Stick" and Blood Work

Immediately after the shot a team of helpers will rush in to accomplish several tasks simultaneously. The team should be careful to stay clear of the pig's feet and legs, which may begin to convulse or kick violently 20-30 seconds after the shot. These convulsions are a natural part of the passing of the animal. The helpers should roll the carcass onto its side and stay on the back side of the animal. Two-three people kneeling on and holding the pig will keep it secure enough for the next steps. One person will be equipped with a boning

knife, or some other long, slender-bladed knife that will be used to "stick" the pig. They should be positioned near the head and will plunge the knife in where the neck joins the body, aiming the tip to find the arteries that pass on both sides of the neck vertebrae. It is not necessary to create a large gaping wound. In fact, the base of the knife, near the handle, need not travel from the point of entry. Rather, the tip of the knife can be moved, raking both sides of the spinal column at the neck.

When successfully done, the flow of blood will be copious and immediate. The shot to the head has rendered the pig senseless, but some of the most basic bodily systems will continue to function for some minutes, including breathing and heartbeat. The blood will flow out in a steady stream for a couple of minutes and is best collected at this point. The person on the team assigned to collect blood will have a large, sterile bowl and a whisk at the ready. After the shot and the "stick", the blood is collected as it pumps from the body simply by holding the bowl up to the flow. The blood should be whisked as soon as it is in the bowl, even as it is being collected. It must be whisked continuously until it cools. This will prevent it from clotting, which it will start doing as soon as it hits the oxygen-rich environment outside the pig's body. As the flow of blood begins to slow, the bowl can be removed to the work area where tables are set up, still whisking all the

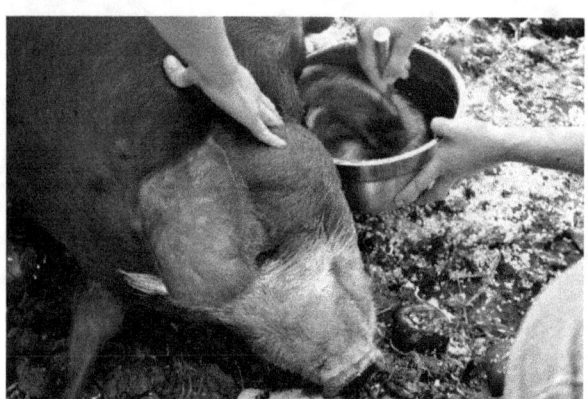

while. When the blood has cooled, pour it through a strainer (to remove any clots that remain) into sterile 1-gallon canning jars. This can be kept refrigerated for up to two weeks before put to use in traditional charcuterie recipes like boudin noir or british-style blood sausage (sometimes called black pudding).

Meanwhile, the team that has been holding the pig still can be working one of the front legs of the pig, pumping it in order to encourage the blood to completely empty the body. Massage the area around the cut vigorously, working the blood out of the wound to prevent clots from forming and stopping the flow. Any auto-responses in the pig will begin to quiet as the blood-flow slows. Be prepared – each death is a little different and a day spent doing this kind of work can take a toll emotionally. It is natural to have grown attached to an animal that you have cared for and raised. Feeling the life exit the animal can evoke feelings of grief and sadness. There is a gravitas in the moment that should not be ignored; this is the cost of our consumption. Take comfort in the knowledge that you have taken the time and effort to ensure that you are not only carrying the full burden of responsibility for the life and death of the animal, but that you have taken measures to makes sure that the pig has died in the most humane manner possible.

When the pig goes completely still, the team can step back and take a breath. An important part of the job is done. If you have killed the pig in a pen where other animals reside, you will probably notice that they are nothing more than curious as the all the activity. And they will be interested in blood as it collects. Pigs are omnivorous and will not hesitate to partake of the spilt blood of their former companions. The carcass of the pig should now be removed from the pen, a task that can be done with sufficient man-power (four capable people, one on each leg) or with mechanical assistance.

We typically use man-power to move the carcass to an area near the scalding tank. Then we engage in a short ritual of appreciation and gratitude for the life of the animal we have just killed. Drams of bourbon are passed out, glasses are raised, a short toast given; as the warmth of the spirit hits our throats and spreads through our core, we turn our attention to the next tasks at hand.

Scald and Scrape

The carcass should be scrubbed clean in preparation for the scald. Several stiff-bristle brushes are useful for this task. After cleaning, the animal can be readied for a gambrel, the device used to suspend the animal while keeping the legs separated. The pig is equipped with a cluster of tendons in  each leg, located just above the trotter, that are capable of holding the weight of the entire pig throughout this process and the hanging of individual sides for butchering. They really are incredible and are easily located. Using the tip of a sharp boning knife, make parallel cuts about 4-5 inches in length and about ½" deep along the back of the leg starting just above the feet. Dig your fingers into the cut and located the thick, corded tendon that runs the length of the leg, it won't be hard to identify. With careful work of fingers and knife-tip, lift a length of the tendon from the bone underneath, so that you can pass your finger through from one cut to the other. Repeat this procedure on all four legs; these will be the cuts that you will pass the gambrel hooks through, and use to suspend sides by the large s-hooks at various times in the process.

Thread the gambrel hooks through the front legs and hook the gambrel to the chain or rope that will raise it above the scalding tank. If you are working with a come-along on a frame or tree, you will need to make sure that the pig does not inadvertently swing into the tank and knock it over. Once it is raised to sufficient height to clear the top of the tank, lower away. If you have the resources and skills to make use of a forklift or tractor, this can be a very convenient way to lift and maneuver a whole pig carcass. In all cases, be especially careful as you maneuver around the scald tank. Be observant of your water level - you don't want water pouring over the sides as you try to lower the pig, nor would it be a good idea to add water after putting the pig in – the temperature would change enough to make it much more difficult to get an ideal scald.

What is an ideal scald? You are aiming to get just over half of the pig fully immersed in the tank at one time. There are a great many theories on scalding out there, but we have

found that the following formula provides a great scald every time. Heat the water to exactly 145F, lower the carcass and leave in the water for exactly 5 minutes. Set a timer, and keep a thermometer handy. Do not let the water temperature rise during that time, or you will move past scalding and onto cooking. Keep the water moving freely around the carcass during the scald, do not allow the pig to rest against the side of the tank or press down on the bottom of the tank. Ideally the pig is suspended in the water. This is one of the reasons that a large volume tank (80-120 gallons) is so much more optimal than a 55-gallon drum. There is just more room to make this work, and a greater volume of water which tends to hold temperatures more stable. Occasionally test the progress of the scald by pulling at hair below the water line – it should pull out easily.

After the five minutes are up, or if your tests reveal that a sufficient scald has been achieved, raise the pig out of the water and move it away from the tank. You 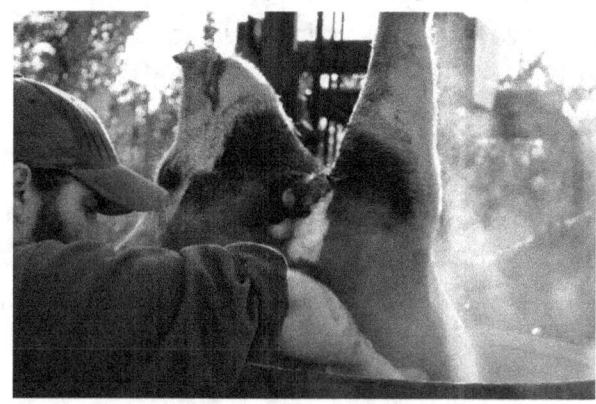 need space for 2-3 people to be able to work on the carcass with scrapers and knives. The scalding process loosens the hair on the body of the pig and the top layer of skin can now be lifted off the carcass. This layer is called the "scurf", and looks something like a peeling sunburn when it comes off. Whatever color your pig was in life (black, brown, red, spotted, etc), it will be pinkish after the scrape is finished.

The scrape needs to be accomplished quickly, as it gets harder as the carcass cools. If you achieve a great scald the result will be a carcass that is easily scraped, a perfect balance of loose scurf but firm flesh beneath. If the temperature was too high or the time too long the carcass will begin to cook, and the hair will "set", making the entire process much, much more difficult. Scrapers tend to gouge and cut the top layer of flesh and the hair does not pull out readily and must be essentially shaved off the carcass. Being exacting about the scald time and temp will make the scraping work much easier, so pay attention to the details.

Scraping is hard work, especially since the pace is pretty demanding. There is not much room around the carcass for many hands, we have found that you can really only have 2-3 people working comfortably. But those people will tire quickly, so other helpers can be waiting in the wings,  ready to step in and provide fresh arms and hands to the process. There are places where the scurf and hair will easily be removed in large swaths, but the carcass has many folds and creases where extra time must be taken to ensure things get clean. Everything must go – the tail can be cleaned, the legs all the way down to the toes must be cleaned of scurf and hair. Where scrapers fail (and they sometimes will), a razor sharp knife can be used to shave areas clean. Be especially careful around your fellow scrapers when wielding a blade. You are going for smooth skin as a finish, so persevere until this is achieved. We have found that even at a brisk pace this can take 30-40 minutes per scald, so don't give up early!

One of the jobs that needs to be done at this stage is the removal of the nails on the trotters. After a good scald, they will likely come off with relative ease, sometimes it is as simple as catching an edge with a scraper and giving a firm tug. But keep a pair of pliers around for stubborn cases.

After scraping the first half completely clean, lower the pig to the ground (we like to keep a couple of clean palettes around as a platform for cleaning and other operations) and move the gambrel from the front legs to the rear. Raise the pig again and scald the second half following the same guidelines as with the first. Be sure to check the temperature of the scald tank before putting the carcass in – if the heat was left on while scraping was going on, the water temp may have risen significantly and you will be very disappointed with the results. 145F for 5min. Raise the carcass and scrape the second half. The head will present a special challenge – get it reasonably clean but it will be in a difficult position for detail work since it will, at this point, be hanging nose-down towards the ground. Work to get the rest of the carcass entirely scraped. When it is done to your satisfaction, rinse the carcass with fresh water, then take brillo pads and vigorously scrub the entire body, top to bottom. Rinse again. The result should be a clean, pink carcass devoid of any hair.

Evisceration

The expression "up to your elbows" is typically used figuratively, to mean one is immersed in a project. In the evisceration of your pig, however, you will find yourself quite literally up to your elbows in the animal. This process will transform your pig from its animal form into clean, ready-for-butchering sides of pork, and will produce some of the most interesting and prized foodstuffs along the way. For many people, though, this is the scary part. They imagine lots of blood, along with vague but unsettling notions of all the stuff that is hiding inside their animal: "guts", organs, tissues, fluids. The truth is far less horrifying than what is imagined: little blood, a well-organized interior, and fresh, firm organs. Instead of the expected "eww" reaction, many folks find themselves uttering "woah...cool" instead.

The tools for this job are few: a sharp 6" boning knife will serve very well for all the cutting work (with one exception that I'll call out below), and a bone saw. While a reciprocating saw can be used, and would certainly be easier on the arms, a sharp, well backed bone saw will cut more cleanly and, more importantly, will track better. You'll enjoy the job more with a couple of helpers to help brace the carcass and take offal away for processing and packaging. And one other thing: a piece of twine, about 12 inches long.

These instructions assume your pig is hanging from a gambrel by both rear legs. Evisceration can be done effectively with the carcass on the ground, but a hanging carcass has several advantages: you'll be working in a more comfortable position, gravity becomes a helping hand for some operations, and it's easier to keep the carcass clean. If you can hang your carcass, do so.

The first task is to remove the head. Imagine a waterline that would be created if you dipped your hanging pig into a pool of water up to the point in the neck where the sticking wound was made. You will be cutting around that imaginary line. Insert your boning knife into the sticking wound, and using long slicing cuts, start working your way around the neck. If your knife is sharp you'll find this to be far easier going than you probably anticipated. Try not to saw your way with little cuts – you want to create a nice smooth surface in the flesh of the neck. The head will hang quite securely from the neck bones as you cut. Work your way all the way around until you've connected the line. You may have to reach in and do some closer cutting up against the neck bones. Once you've reached bone all the way around the neck, you will need to crack the neck bones in order to completely sever the neck. This is a good job for a helper, who can grab both ears and twist the head around until there is an audible crack, and a feeling of something giving way. At this point your helper should be able to pull the head up and away from the body, while you reach in with your knife to sever any last tissues that remain connected. The head will come free, and should be taken away for careful cleaning, described in detail in another section.

The next task is to cut the rectum free. The goal is to free the rectum to the extent that it can be pulled out far enough to get tied closed with a piece of strong twine. Doing so ensures no feces will make its way out, contaminating the body cavity. You may need to be up on a stepladder to do this work, depending on the hanging height of your carcass. Be sure to have secure footing while working with your knife.

It's helpful to imagine the rectum and vagina of the pig as being encased in a heavy hose, with thick walls. You will be trying to cut around the outside of that hose.

To start your cut, lift the tail with one hand and insert the knife, blade parallel to the walls of the imaginary hose, just below the tail. Try to feel your way along the bones of the tail, keeping the knife gliding right up along those bones. Use the full length of the blade.

Now that you're in, you'll work your way around the anus and vulva, keeping the knife cutting along the walls of

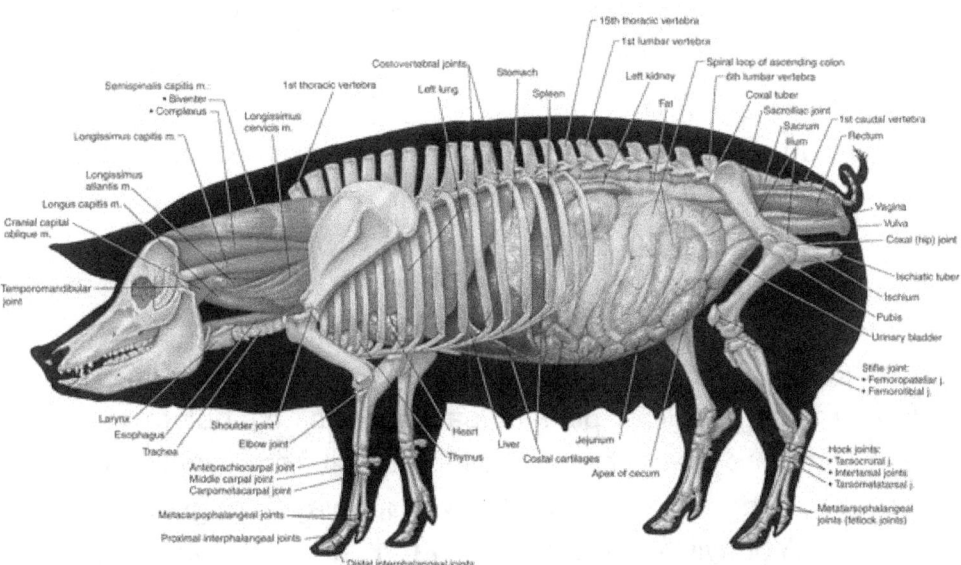

your imaginary hose, and keeping a uniform distance away from the anus. You can angle the tip of the knife away from the hose as you cut. Imagine that you are working your knife around the top of a traffic cone. Pinch the flap of flesh of the vulva, or "gilt", with one hand while you work your knife around

with the other. This is an
awkward position, but it helps
avoid the rectum retreating into
the body once you've cut it free.

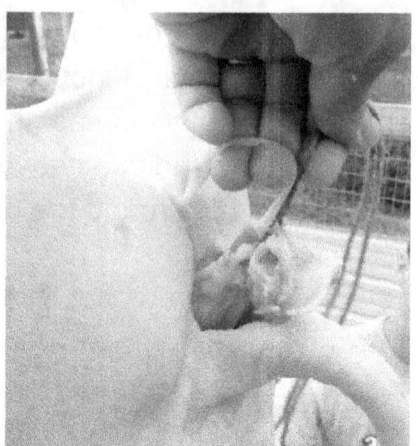

If all goes well you will be
able to get your hand around
the walls of the rectum, and you
can pull it out a few inches.
Don't worry about breaking
anything – this is strong tissue! But you might have someone
standing by with some paper towels or wet wipes in the event
that some fecal matter works its way out while you are
working. Once you have a few inches of the hose exposed,
tie it off firmly with a length of twine. Once tied off you can let
it be.

You need to get the sternum split open next, and you
will use your knife and the bone saw for that. Start an incision
at the neck and cut up along the center of the carcass. You
will feel the sternum just under the surface of the skin. When
you reach the end of the sternum, stop your cut. Hold the saw
with the handle high, the tip low, and use just the tip of the
blade, making shallow, pushing saw strokes. It's helpful to
have someone brace the carcass to keep it from spinning or
swaying during this operation. Saw your way through the
sternum. You will feel it give way when you are through the
bone – stop sawing immediately when this occurs.

With the rectum tied off and the sternum split, you're
ready to open up the belly. The goal is to get an opening
started that will then allow you to work from the inside of the

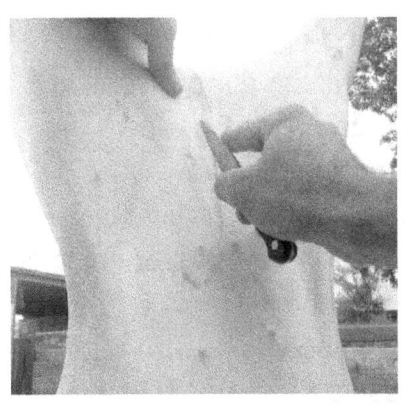

belly. You must work carefully, to avoid puncturing the intestines or stomach. With the pig hanging the stomach and intestines are themselves sagging downward, which creates a bit of a pocket for you to start. Find the centerline of the animal, between the rear legs – this is where you will slice in, creating a vertical incision some 6 inches long. Pretend to be a surgeon, using careful, precise movements. Don't try to cut all the way through in one go. Instead, try to intentionally and lightly slice through a single layer at a time. You have three distinct layers to work through: first the skin, then the fat, and finally the viscera, the tissue wall of the lower body cavity. Be particularly careful in this last layer, as you create a small hole into which you can get a finger or a hand pushed through. Now you will be able to pull the skin out and away from the intestines, and open the slice up a bit more.

Once you have enough of an opening to get your hand into the body cavity, you will be able to start cutting from the inside. Get your non-knife hand in the body cavity, fingers pointed down towards the ground and palm pressed against the inside of the belly. You'll feel the firm, ropy intestines against the back of your hand. You'll use your hand as a shield to keep the intestines away from the knife. Press the back of your hand into the intestines, and cup your hand to create a pocket. Bring the knife in, with the back of

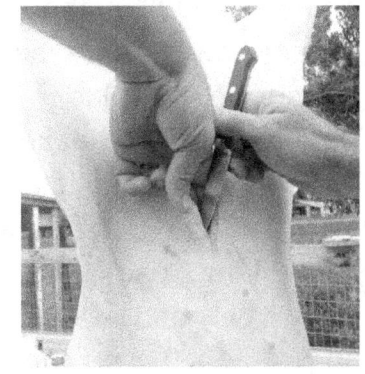

the knife against the heel of your cupped hand, and the tip protected inside the pocket. The knife will be almost vertical, not horizontal. Now move this whole arrangement down the belly. Your cupped hand will keep the intestines away from the blade, and you will simultaneously apply pressure to the back of the knife as you slice downwards. When everything is working the belly will slice open like a zippered jacket. The intestines will keep trying to assert themselves as you cut further and further down. Keep pressing them back, using your forearm and elbow. Remember that part about being in up to your elbows? Well, this is it. Keep going until you reach the opening you made at the sternum.

If you accidentally puncture or slice the intestines or stomach don't worry. You'll have to put up with some unhappy smells, and you'll have more cleaning go do when you're done, but keep moving and you'll get through it.

A shorter knife would be easier than your boning knife for this operation. Easier still would be a large gut hook. This specialty blade is made to do exactly this task. You can acquire one as part of a large game cleaning kit.

The pig carcass is now ready to be emptied of its contents, now that that you've opened the belly and chest. What follows is the systematic removal of those contents, harvesting along the way. Have a large bin ready to receive the parts you are not keeping, and some clean receptacles for the offal you intend to keep.

First, reach up and grab the rectum from inside the body cavity and pull the tied off hose out through the body, letting it hang outside the carcass. There may be some tough connective tissue that creates resistance, you can work with fingers or very carefully with a knife to free things up. Start spilling the large and small intestines out of the cavity. You are creating space to work. The small intestines can be taken and freed from their connective tissues, flushed thoroughly with clean water, and stored for later processing. Find the lobes of the liver, deep brown/red, and gently move them aside until you find the large blood vessels connected to the liver. Cut them, and pull the liver out. Cut the green sac of the gall bladder off the liver (being extremely careful not to puncture it), and discard it. Hand the liver off to a helper to rinse it and store it away.

You need to expose the stomach, which will be lying underneath the intestines. Find the large, smooth bag of the stomach. Feel your way around to the far side of the stomach until you can feel the esophagus, which exits the stomach and travels through the diaphragm and to the throat. Feel your way down the esophagus, grab hold of it tightly, and pull. Pull hard, and pull steady, and you will pull the esophagus out of the throat. With that, you've freed up both ends of the digestives system and you will be able to spill all of it out into a waiting bin. If you are harvesting intestines for casings, or stomach for tripe, do so now. Find the long, pink, marbled organ – the spleen. Harvest the delicate and lacy caul fat attached to it, and harvest the spleen itself.

The respiratory and circulatory systems are next. First, cut the diaphragm away, leaving the thin muscles along the rib cage but removing the tissue of the diaphragm. Reaching down past the lungs and feel your way to the ribbed trachea.

Feel as far along it as you can, then grab it firmly and pull it out of the throat. You'll be able to pull the heart and lungs right out with it. Cut the heart free and set aside for harvest. Do the same with the lungs.

Turn your attention back to the now almost empty body cavity. You will find two small muscles hanging down from the spine…the "hanging tenders". You may opt to cut these free now and hand them to your helper, who, if properly prepared, could cook them up fast in a hot pan for a post evisceration snack. But you still have work to do.

Finish the knife work on the outside of the carcass, extending the initial incision back to the hole where you removed the rectum. Cut until you hit the pelvic bone. Reach inside the carcass, and score the tissue that covers the spine, slicing a line down the spine that you'll use as a cutting guide for splitting the carcass.

Switch to the saw for the splitting. Your goal is to cut the carcass perfectly in half along the spine. Stand facing the belly, and start by doing a quick bit of sawing through the front of the pelvic bone. Have a helper hold the tail to one side, line up your saw on the center line, and start sawing with long, controlled strokes. Let the saw do the work. Keep yourself square to the body, and try to get a perfectly even split of the ridge bones that extend from the spine to the back. Your helpers can brace the carcass, and help spread the halves as you make progress down the spine. Keep going, all the way through the neck. This will tire you out, but you are almost done. As you reach the neck, your helping hands can steady the halves on the gambrel so they don't swing as you complete the cut.

Stand back, stretch, then give the halves a good rinse. They are ready to be cooled down overnight, and you should be ready for a quick taste of those pan-fried tenders before you start cleaning up your tools and your site.

Head Work

It is a real shame that the pig head is so underappreciated as a culinary object. There are really incredible dishes that use some or all of the head, but it is not commonplace these days to see the head as food. The temptation, therefore, is to pay little attention to it, instead viewing it as one of the undesirable cast-offs of the process. Do not make this mistake! Take care to treat the head as food, and you will be rewarded richly in the end.

The head is removed from the body early in the evisceration stage. Have a bus tub or similar sized tray available to hold the head and a helper who will be assigned to clean it up for roasting or butchering. The head has many folds and flaps of skin that make scraping it a particularly difficult task and no doubt there will be hair left where the scrapers failed. But it must be rendered as clean as the rest of the carcass – this is detail work and should be done with some patience. Tools for this job include a bell scraper, brillo pads, disposable razors, and a boning knife.

The only cut that need be done is to remove the ear canal from each ear. This is done with the boning knife, working around the curled and coiled cartilage of the ear, coring it as one would core an apple. The cartilage can be removed and a smooth car is left. Hair should be scraped from all parts of the head, with the goal being to make the head as absolutely clean as possible. The razor and knife can be used in close work where the scraper won't be effective. Scrub the head with a brillo pad and rinse when the work is completed.

The head can be roasted whole (a dramatic and tasty treat for a harvest dinner), or can be divided and harvested. The jowels (cheeks) of the pig are especially valuable and can be easily cured (resulting in guanciale, an Italian kitchen staple) or used for high-end sausage or salami recipes, since the fat is particularly silky. The entire head can be put into a brining bucket in preparation for making head cheese, a really delicious dish that suffers from a truly unfortunate name.

Keeping Things Cool

At the end of the first day, your pig will have undergone a significant transformation and the clean sides of pork that you are left with now more closely resemble meat than they do a snuffling and snorting pig. The cleaned head and sides now need to be quickly and completely chilled. Unlike beef, pork does not benefit from aging, but it does need to be chilled in order to protect the meat from spoiling. This will also firm it up the flesh and fat, making butchering a much more pleasant task.

If you are fortunate enough to live in a cold-weather climate you can plan your harvest for the late fall or early winter months and take advantage of ambient temperatures between 20-40 degrees F. In such conditions the sides can be left to hang overnight outside or in an uninsulated building. You do not want the sides to freeze, rather they should be chilled through to the bone. Our first year of harvest saw ideal outside temps and our sides were perfectly chilled after a hanging over night – we even woke to find them dusted with a fresh coating of snow.

However, weather can be hard to count on and in some regions such temperatures are a rare occurrence. Do not be discouraged! There are a variety of options available, ranging from simple to quite involved. The most direct would be to bury the sides in ice, utilizing a water trough or plastic kiddie pool to handle the size your are working with.

It might be the case that you can gain access to a cold room in your area where you can hang your pork until well chilled. Butcher shops, small grocery stores, beverage distributers, etc. – all are options to explore, and a phone call and a case of beer may be all that is required to borrow some space.

But, if you want to really step up your home-harvest game, you might consider building your own cold storage space. We did just that, constructing what is essentially a well-insulated box that is cooled by use of a window-mounted air-conditioning unit. The ac unit is controlled by use of an override device that allows it to cool well below its normal range, resulting in a walk-in cooler that can be put together for a pretty modest cost. It can be built in a basement, a garage, or even as a freestanding outbuilding. And the temperature is adjustable so that the same space can do duty as a cheese room or produce cellar.

Good information on construction of a cold room can be found at www.storeitcold.com.

Basics of Side Butchery

One of the side-affects of the development of the industrialized food system is the way general knowledge is transformed into specialized knowledge and common jobs become professional jobs. Farming has become centralized into mass, monolithic operations and so the home garden, in all of its varied glory, gives way to the industrial farm planted with thousands of acres of corn. This allows for incredible efficiency of production, since operators can focus on one product. But it also means that the general knowledge of how to grow things is lost as we hand over production to specialists. The same effect is felt in meat production. Historically, a smallholder might have a pig or two as part of the diverse manner of providing for self, family and community, and would have been quite capable of making good use of the whole of the harvest. Today we have a few pig farmers and hordes of grocery shoppers, and the knowledge of what meat is and where it comes from is left to professionals. The job of butchering, which is simply the portioning of an animal into cuts suitable for home use, has left the home kitchen and has developed into a job carried on by mysterious persons in white coats, working behind closed doors.

It is not our intent, by any means, to denigrate the job of the butcher. There is a vast body of knowledge that takes years of practice to acquire. But we have been surprised by how achievable good results are at home with just a small selection of tools and some general guidance. You can do this! A pig is a wonder of food efficiency, with nearly every bit of it holding the potential to wind up as delicious and interesting food. The only real mistake one can make would be to fail to use all of what the pig has given.

Our approach here is not to present a comprehensive guide to side butchery. Rather we want to give the reader a good start on this exciting job and point you in the direction of additional resources that will help you make the most of your harvest. We are deeply indebted to the work of artisan butcher and teacher Brandon Sheard for getting us started with cutting our own meat. Brandon and his wife Lauren are

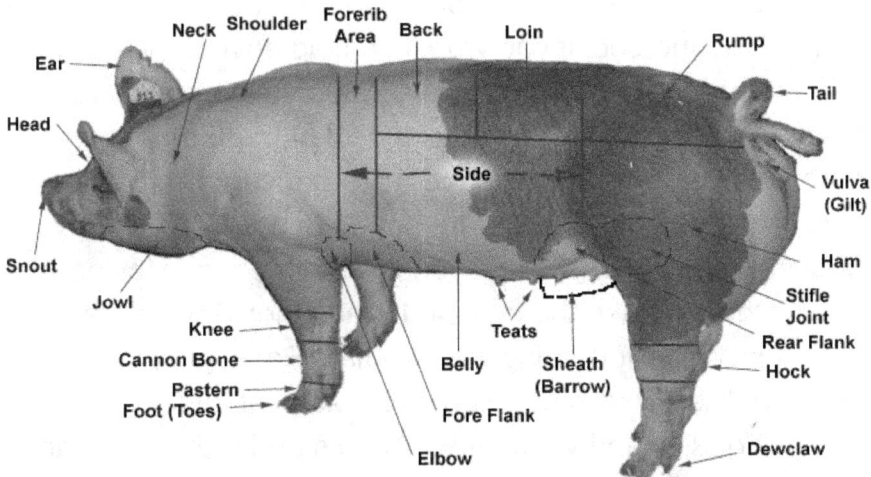

the visionaries behind www.farmsteadmeatsmith.com and they have made it their mission to put the skills of home harvest in the hands of anyone who desires to learn. Having had the opportunity to learn from Brandon, we can attest to the value of hands-on training. They have also made some wonderful videos on side butchery and harvest choices that are available on their website. Anyone who chooses to investigate the topic of butchery more thoroughly would do well to start there.

Space

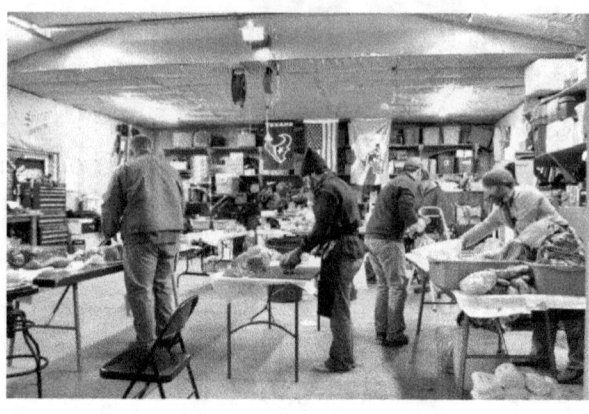

All that is really required is a well-lit, large horizontal surface upon which to work. It is convenient to have good lighting and access to clean hot and cold water. The ambient temperature of the space is a consideration as well. Your pork will stay firm and cool if you work in a cold environment like an unheated garage or shop. But you can also work indoors, you will just want to take steps to make cold storage a possibility for the sides and for the cuts you will produce. It will make the job go much smoother if you are set up to wrap and label your product at the same time that you are butchering. Having helpers who can take the cuts and ready them for the freezer or set them aside for curing is essential. Packaging the product well is a vital step to ensure that all of your meat retains its quality and value in the weeks and months ahead.

We have butchered as many as eight sides at a time, using long, sturdy tables as our work surfaces and utilizing the labor of friends and family to help the job go as smoothly as possible. Working in teams, one person works the knives while another attends to wrapping. Once again, the harvest is an opportunity for community to come together and enjoy some shared labor.

You must be prepared to store all of the chops and roasts that you will soon be in possession of – think ahead and have freezer space ready.

Tools & Equipment

6" boning knife
10" long knife (straight steak, cimeter, or other)
Large cleaver
Bone saw
Knife sharpener

Large Cutting Board

Plastic Wrap & Butcher paper
Or
Vacuum seal equipment

2-gallon Ziploc bags
2 5-gallon food grade buckets

Several clean bus tubs

Initial Steps

Lay one side on a clean work surface with the skin side down and the legs facing you. There are a few steps that need to be done before the side is divided into quarters.

Hanging Tender: You will begin by first trimming the hanging tenders (you may have done this on harvest day if you went for pork tacos). This muscle lies in the middle of the body cavity and is covered on both sides by a sturdy membrane. Slide the knife close to the body and remove the tender. Using fingers and knife, work the membrane off of the meat. The resulting cut is a great BBQ piece, responding well to flash cooking over high heat.

Kidneys: It is possible that the kidneys were left in the sides, as they are sometimes missed during evisceration. They are protected in a layer of fat, and can be cut free and removed at this time.

Leaf Fat: There are several kinds of fat on a pig, each having different qualities and uses. The leaf fat lines the inside of the body cavity, a creamy white covering that, when rendered, produces high-quality lard. It can be removed by working fingers

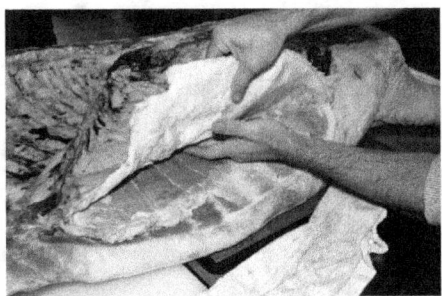

under the leading edge (nearer the head) and pulling it out. This will require some force, but it will separate from the side without the need for a knife. The sheet of fat can be diced and cooked over very low heat and the resulting liquid fat ladled into jars. It will cool into a snow-white creamy lard, useful for frying or baking in the kitchen.

Tenderloin: Working with your fingers and a knife, separate the tenderloin from the side. It is tucked up next to the spine and surrounded by some tough connective tissue. Once you have worked it most of the way out, cut it free.

Four Quarters

It can feel overwhelming to face the whole side of pork, but the reality is that a side will be divided into much more manageable and logical portions. These are called "quarters", as there are four of them: belly, loin, shoulder, and leg. Terminology sometimes varies between traditions, so do not take our choice of language here to be exclusive. We will first give steps to divide into quarters, and then focus on some of the cuts you might expect from each one.

Leg quarter: The "leg" in the leg quarter refers to the rear leg of the pig. Locate the spine and follow it down from the tail. It will make a sharp and distinct turn upward – from that turn count two more vertebrae towards the head. This will be the point of separation. Cut the carcass smoothly, avoid a lot of slicing motions – rather let the large knife scribe a straight line top to bottom . You will be left with the spine only, there are no other bones to hinder your cut. Flip the leg up and fold the quarter over on top of the rest of the side. A sharp crack will let you know that the spine has broken, and a quick slip of the knife will free it from the side.

Shoulder quarter: This is the front leg of the pig and is the source for meat that is well-marbled with fat, perfect for roasts or for sausage. Find the end of the sternum, there will be a piece of cartilage that tapers to an end at the front end of the belly. Starting there, draw a line through to the spine, using the ribs as a natural guide. Connect a cut around the back and to the spine from the top. You may find that there are some flat, thin bones that prevent a direct cut to the spine. These are called feather bones – use the boning knife to slip behind them, cutting back in towards the place where your cuts intersect the spine. Fold the quarter over and on top of the loin and belly, listening again for the sharp crack that lets you know you are nearly done. Cut remaining tissue with the knife and remove the quarter.

Loin & Belly quarters: The belly and loin quarters comprise the center section of the side and will now be separated. Turn the entire section on end and you will see the pork chops revealed in profile. Pick a spot where you'd like the chops to end and score the skin there. Turn to the other end and do the same. Now lay it flat, skin side up and use the boning knife to connect the two hash marks, cutting all the way through the belly. When the knife meets the ribs, slide up and cross over the top, cutting down into the gaps. You will then need to finish the task with the bone saw, nipping through the ribs one by one.

Basic Cuts

From the belly –
Filet the ribs off of the
belly, working close to
the bone. The rack of
ribs can be set aside
for summer BBQ. The
remaining panel can be cut into two or three rectangles.
These can be made into bacon, pancetta, etc. – rub them with
a cure immediately and slip them into 2-gallon Ziploc bags.
They will cure in the fridge for about a week before heading for
the smoker, oven, or other steps.

From the loin – First find the seam between the backfat
and the topfat on the ribs. You will see a visible line
separating the two layers, it runs along the loin quarter
between the skin and the top of the ribs. Work your fingers
into this seam, applying pressure inward and downward. The
backfat will work off, sometimes with ease, at times with
difficulty, but don't give up! This special fat is essential for
salami and sausage, or it can be cured itself into a product
called "lardo." This layer is nearly impossible to preserve
when the carcass is skinned, so much of the fat is lost along
with the skin. Your hard work scalding and scraping really
pays off here! Remove the backfat and set aside, it can be
frozen for later use.

Next, begin on the rib end and use a knife to cut
between ribs down to the spine. At the bottom you will need
to use a cleaver to finish the cut through the bone. Then lay
the separated chop on the board and use the cleaver again to

cut the chine bone piece off of the corner of the chop. After the chops are removed, carefully filet the spine off of the remaining loin. You can then isolate and remove the loin muscle for a boneless loin roast, or crosscut the loin into thin boneless chops.

From the leg – Cut the trotter off, scoring around the leg and using the saw to finish the cut through. Save for soup, stock, pickling or roasting. Cut the tail where it joins the spine, save for a slow-roasted treat. Decide upon your basic approach to the leg, whether you desire cured ham, dry-aged prosciutto, or roasts. You may want to cut the hock, or leave it depending on your use. If so, cut meat with the knife and finish bone with the saw. If you desire a whole leg for dry-curing (this is an ambitious project), you will leave much of the hock intact and separate the leg at the ball join in the pelvis, working carefully with your boning knife. In most cases you will likely go for a traditional ham, which can be achieved by cutting down to the femur with the knife, then finishing that substantial bone with the saw. Complete the cut with the knife and set the ham aside for brining.

The rest of the leg can be turned into sirloin roasts, bone-in or boneless, or is an excellent source of well-marbled meat for sausage. We have found that 3lb-5lb roasts are an excellent and versatile product. They are easily packaged and provide great flexibility for the average family, as they can be roasted whole, cubed for pulled pork, or ground for sausage at a later date. Farmstead Meatsmith has produced an excellent how-to video on side butchery that provides a walk-through on pulling roasts from the leg quarter, it can be found at www.farmsteadmeatsmith.com

From the shoulder – The shoulder is an excellent source of fat-infused meat that has a nearly perfect ratio for sausage. By nature of this fat, it also makes for excellent whole roasts. When slow-cooked in low heat, the fat renders into the meat delivering deep flavor and preserving moisture. First remove the trotter by bending the foot and finding the second knuckle in the leg. While maintaining pressure on the leg, score around the joint with a knife, then work through the connecting tendons. The trotter will come away without the need for a saw. Cross-cut the hock up to where it joins the body, scoring with a knife and finishing the cut with a saw. You might create smaller sections in order to make smoked hocks later, or decide to take the hock in one piece (it can be braised for a delicious meal).

You may need to use the saw to cut across the ends of the shoulder ribs, then filet them off of the shoulder. At this point you will notice some dark blood clots lining the wound caused by the "sticking" of the pig during slaughter. These clots, and any meat that has been "burned" by this blood, need to be trimmed out and discarded. You can see now the value of creating a relatively small wound during bleed-out, more meat is preserved for harvest.

One of the simplest approaches at this point is to divide the remaining quarter roughly in half, top and bottom, cutting through the shoulder-blade with a saw when it is encountered. Those halves can then be divided into roasts, and any trimmings set aside for sausage. The roasts can be deboned at this time, with careful work of the knife, and the bones set aside for stock. The shoulder blade is a tricky piece to work around the first time, as it is hard to visualize how it lays in the meat. But don't' fret, you can't make any terminal mistakes here, if the roasts do not turn out, simply set the meat aside for sausage.

Preserving the Harvest

There are infinite possibilities for making the most of your harvest, but some short discussion on a few of the common approaches will be of use. We've organized this section based upon generalized preservation technique – specific recipes are far too numerous to include, but our suggested reading at the end is a good place to begin researching.

Fresh

There is too much pork in one pig to consider keeping it all fresh, but there are some products that are best utilized right away and because of their delicacy and/or short shelf life should be prepared in short order.

Blood – Pig blood is used in several important cultural recipes, including black pudding and boudin noir. Once harvested, it can be kept cold in a fridge for two weeks or so. Blood sausage is a rich and delicious meal that will come to be associated with harvest time since it is best made and consumed within a few weeks.

Head – The head should be dealt with immediately after harvest. After taking the jowels for sausage or curing, the entire head can be placed in a brine and then boiled in order to produce head cheese. Or the entire head can be slow-roasted at low heat, then finished at 500F to crisp the skin and fat near the surface. It is a dramatic presentation that is also a wonderful family-style meal, as the meat can be pulled off from just about anywhere. Don't let the head go to waste, there is a great deal of nutritious and delicious meat tucked into this overlooked cut.

Offal – Patè is a wonderful and rich use of pork liver, and there are many possibilities for fancy or country combinations. Having some of this made at harvest time can add a touch of class to your harvest dinner and will introduce some of your guests to a food experience that will be sure to excite. Some recipes are designed to be preserved by canning.

Included in this category are the intestines, which can be flushed clean and then processed for sausage casings. It is a rather involved task – they are turned inside out and scraped clean of their lining. It is not particularly pleasant work, but the resulting casings are superior to their manufactured counterparts. Clean casings can be stored in salt nearly indefinitely. Soak in several changes of clean water to prepare them for use.

Frozen

It is so very easy and convenient to deep-freeze food in the home, and anyone contemplating harvesting a whole or half pig should invest in a chest-style freezer. Most of your product will end up here for some time, so packaging for freezer storage is one of the most important aspects of the harvest. We have found that vacuum-sealing is pretty hard to beat in terms of the quality that is protected and preserved. Invest in a quality unit and you will find yourself surprised by how often you will use it for all kinds of food storage. But vacuum seal units are not always available or affordable – as an alternative, product can be tightly wrapped in plastic wrap and then butcher paper. Be sure to label your packages well, since you will soon forget which cut is which when faced with a freezer full of neat white bundles.

Packaging for the freezer should be done while butchering is ongoing. Once you get comfortable with side butchery, you will find that it is the packaging step is actually more time consuming, so having the work going on concurrent with cutting will ensure that your meat is preserved at its most fresh.

Curing & Smoking

This is where things get really exciting. Curing is pretty simply defined as preserving meat, usually by means of adding salt. Variations on this include the addition of nitrates or nitrites, sugar and spices. The most common products that undergo some sort of curing are bacon and ham, and if those are all that you ventured to try you would certainly be happy with the results. However, there are also easy-to-achieve products that you can make at home, products you may not be as familiar with, like guanciale or lardo. Once you start experimenting, you will find yourself amazed at the quality and variety of food you can make using curing techniques. Adding smoke to the curing process can bring yet another striking layer of flavor to the party.

Curing does introduce one to the raging debate over the health issues surrounding the use of nitrates and nitrites in the preservation process. These compounds are used to ensure that deadly botulism spores do not gain a foothold in your salami or ham. There are some health concerns linked to nitrates, and anyone using or even storing these compounds in their home needs to be well-informed as to the hazards they represent (nitrates are often sold as "pink salt", and in this form they resemble colored sugar – a tempting sight for children who don't know that the substance is poison when ingested in large portions). But, despite these risks, they do bring great benefit and peace of mind when used appropriately. Take time to study the issues and come to your own decision about the use of nitrates in the preservation of the food you will feed yourself and your family.

There has been something of a renaissance in preserved meats of late, and there are, as a result, several great books available to those who wish to try their hand at this. We can recommend two by authors Michael Ruhlman and Brian Polcyn: Charcuterie: The Craft of Salting, Smoking, & Curing and Salumi: The Craft of Italian Dry-Curing. These texts represent the tip of the proverbial iceberg, but will introduce the curious cook to the techniques required for great results.

Afterward

By the end of it all, your arms and back will be sore, a deep tired will be on you. The whole process is a big work, as one might expect. But it is deeply satisfying work. We have found that our choice to take on this work for ourselves has resulted in a deepened respect and appreciation for our animals, and a sense of confidence in our own ability to gain some control over the ways and means of acquiring the food that we feed ourselves, our families, and our community. But the decision to engage in this work arises out of far more than an economic argument and it is bigger than a nostalgic look back to days past. It demands a commitment to community life, to hospitality, to stewardship and to generosity. The commitment to these values goes beyond a claim on them as the niceties of society - they are vital, necessary, and needful.

That may all sound a bit high-minded for a discussion about harvesting a pig. But this process highlights a kind of connectedness: our connections to one another, our connections to food and to the animals we take it from, to the land that we take it from. These connections have all been weakened in our contemporary culture of commoditization. The plastic wrapped packages of meat we buy in the store, or the neatly arranged piles of fruits or vegetables soaking under the misters in the produce aisle, these are far removed from their places and processes of origin. Regaining a connection to our food is a way to not only regain control over the quality and economics of our food, but also a way to explore the reforging of those connective paths between our food and each other.

If you take up this work, you will be forced, also, to confront the full cost of your food consumption. The price of this bounty was the life of a pig, a pig that you, perhaps, took the time to raise and nurture. We are not faced with this fact in the grocery store, or the restaurant, and the distance between the harvest and the plate can make us overly casual in what we consume. Applying creative use of the entirety of the pig is not just good eats, it is an ethical imperative – waste would be inappropriate in the face of the cost of the bounty we receive. It is a sobering reality that also grows our appreciation and our gratitude.

Harvest is meant to be a seasonal pursuit, it is part of a cycle, a repeating loop of sowing and reaping. Taking part in the harvest of an animal is serious stuff and despite the bounteous provision that comes from it, it is not uncommon to feel a heaviness and a longing for the birth/nurture cycle to begin again. Gazing out over a now-empty pasture after the harvest is complete will make the mind race forward to spring, when young pigs will once again root and run through the grass. In the meantime, make full use of everything that the pig has given, share what you have and cultivate in others the appreciation that you have found for the noble pig.

Additional Resources

A resource site developed for this book is available at www.harvestingathome.net. There you will find specific recommendations on tools and equipment, stories of harvest, pictures and discussions, as well as the ability to send your particular questions to the authors. Come by and visit! We can also recommend the following:

Suggested Reading

Charcuterie: The Craft of Salting, Smoking, and Curing; by Brian Polcyn and Michael Ruhlman

Pork & Sons; by Stéphane Reynaud

Salumi: The Art of Italian Dry-Curing; by Brian Polcyn and Michael Ruhlman

The Whole Beast: Nose to Tail Eating; by Fergus Henderson

Whole Beast Butchery: The Complete Visual Guide to Beef, Lamb and Pork; by Ryan Farr

Web Resources

www.farmsteadmeatsmith.com

www.butcherpacker.com

www.storeitcold.com

www.ingramcontent.com/pod-product-compliance
Lightning Source LLC
Chambersburg PA
CBHW070817290526
45795CB00002B/745